Salt & Light

Michelle Young

For getting through the storm

SECTIONS

ACKNOWLEDGMENTS

I would like to thank my family for their support, recommendations and late night edits getting ready to publish this book. A special thank you to my husband for pushing me to complete this book the way I have dreamed it should look like. I would also like to thank the readers who picked up this book and hope you find encouragement and a little bit of yourself in these words. My wish is that these words help you as they have helped me.

SALT

Desperation has settled in
and moved into our house.
Every setback starts a different disaster.
A new tornado,
ripping up trees
and their roots;
blowing out windows,
shattering dreams.

Our house is a dark, miserable place,
where happiness goes to die.
We live here,
but it's killing us.

-Infertility journey

You think too much he said.
But who can I talk to,
when no one wants to hear
what is left unsaid?

Michelle Young

It's only once you're gone
that people notice things you've done.

I've got so much to say,
but the sound won't come out of my mouth.
Suffocating under my own breath,
I try to scream but all I hear is silence.

You held me captive,
but told me I was free.
Then you let me go,
but said I was yours.

-Tug of war

My ears bleed the words you said;
too much wrong crowding my head.

You asked to see the real me,
so I showed you my scars
and shared my story.
You looked away
and said I was ugly.

-So-called friends

You hurt me so deep,
it swallowed me whole.
I turned away from you,
so I no longer needed to face you.
You tried to win me back,
with nice comments about this and that,
but my trust you no longer keep,
where you dug a big hole under my feet.

-Fooled me twice

I have trust issues.
I'm not sure how to react
when people say nice things to me,
I watch their smile
and smile back;
but all the while,
listen for their lie.

I smile because
that's what people want
and because I want to see
if I still can.

As hard as I try, I can't save myself.
I look at my reflection in the struggles,
stranded alone in this pool of blackness.
Darkness floods over, until all I see is sadness.
Too weak to fight my own battles,
I guess it's time to just accept my fate.

I don't accept favors.
I don't want to owe anyone anything.
Most people expect something back,
when they extend their empty hand.

I smile in public,
because that's what's expected of me.
If they ever saw what I'm hiding inside,
they wouldn't come near me.

When the power goes out in your house,
you hear every noise it makes.
Like a body that is sick,
feels every organ.

I find it difficult to make decisions,
because every time I've made one,
people have judged me and discouraged me.
So I ask them what my next step should be,
but they tell me they don't know my dreams,
so they can't help me.

-I give others all the power

Like a deer within the trees,
I blend into the weeds.
I can make myself invisible
and it's entirely possible
that you've been walking alongside me,
without ever noticing me.

No matter how much time goes by,
I realize I'm never going to be
completely free.
You will always be
the worst part of me.

Michelle Young

My oldest friend,
the one that knows me best,
lives inside my head
and whispers lies I'm beginning to trust.

The worst thing you ever did to me wasn't:

the abuse,
the lying,
the blackmailing,
the bullying,
the manipulating,
the crying,
the isolating,

but making me believe I was worthless and ordinary.

Michelle Young

He loved me for my body
and the things he could see.
But I wanted one of a kind,
one who would love me for my mind.

I'm never the star of the show,
the one people came out to see.
I'm just the middle act,
they didn't know would make them laugh.

Michelle Young

A heavy sky pours out rain
onto dry earth not prepared
to deal with the flooding
the clouds will leave behind.

Inside my head there's lots of noise,
lots of gray and lots of holes.

I feel myself going deeper into the dark place,
considering how to end it.
I know this place too well;
I've come back here often.
It's a strangely comforting place,
but it's not the right place for me to be.

The walls in my bedroom are infected with the memory and the pain he's caused me. The poison of his words leaks out of the cracks in the ceiling, like a roof leak during a heavy rain. I can't keep living like this - a prisoner in my own home. Trapped like a caged dog, waiting to be released by its master. I don't belong to him anymore; I never did. He should not have any power over me, I'm free. But am I really? The chains have been cut, but they left scars.

His fingerprints are tattooed all over my skin where he marked his territory, sucking the last drop of life out of me.

Nothing
is as disappointing
as an unmet expectation.

Sometimes, I wish
I'd broken my leg instead
of getting lost in my head.

People see a broken leg
and help to hold you up
when you're too weak
to stand.
But no one lends a hand,
to those too destroyed to speak.

-Depression

Sleep comes easy at night.
It's when I wake,
that I must face my demons.

You were holding on tight,
when she was near
and pushing her away,
when she was already gone.

I often stumble
down the road
ahead of me,
because I cannot see clearly
what plans lay there for me.

You couldn't just let me have this,
this happiness.

You had to come back
and take it away.
Like it was a borrowed gift;
something you could take back.
But I had found it on my own,
it was not yours to give.

Michelle Young

I tried to find myself
in everyone else,
but I lost myself
in the process.

Water splashes my face,
but it still doesn't erase,
the times of regret;
those that I can't forget.
The times I gave up,
the chances I passed up,
words I never spoke up,
apologies I never wrote up.

The thing is,
I learned to become comfortable here
in this place.
I learned to push everyone out
of this space.

Even when people are knocking to come inside,
I shut the curtains and hide.

How can you hear what I'm saying,
when you're constantly interrupting?
You can't do much hearing,
when you're doing all the talking.

We were together on that boat,
but when you started the engine,
I fell out and fought against the currant.
You made waves as you picked up speed.
They covered me whole
and I started sinking deep.

Being happy
doesn't come naturally to me.
It's something I'm consciously and continuously
working very hard
to appear natural at.

My future is about as clear
as an unfocused microscope.

Don't ask me
how I'm doing,
unless you're willing
to pick up the pieces
I'll be laying.

How can I forget someone
who destroyed
the girl
I thought I was?

Your compliments are like:
handing me a blanket for my feet
when it's my arms that are cold.

We're growing more and more sophisticated.
We spit out words with so much hatred.

Why do we let these things come between us?
We should be grateful for all God has blessed upon us.
Instead we stare at our empty hands,
and look up to the sky to place our demands.

I keep drawing my bow,
my words hit like an arrow,
right in your heart where my poison spreads.
It's too late for me, it's already infected my head.

The rejection is getting to be too much for me to handle.
You say you'll be there for me like a vigil candle.
But my pain and disappointment can't seem to hide,
the gray skies that are covering my eyes.

I have a knife stabbing my heart,
but I just can't seem to die.
I can't breathe
but I constantly look for air.

-Breaking up

Sometimes I wonder,
why I let him talk to me this way
and I have fantasies about blocking him
out of my life for good.
But there's something about his abusive words
that is familiar to me
and I just can't cut myself off of it.
It's like an addiction,
when you know it's bad for you
but you do it anyway.

He treats me well
and I dream of going back to him.
But I know it's all a lie,
because minutes later,
he starts up again.
I think this is the only way
we really know how to be with each other.
I know it's not healthy
but I can't stop.

It's like his words
have become part of who I am.

I don't know who I am,
without him there to remind me.
Without him, I'm invisible.

I'd rather be in pain than invisible.

-Addicted to pain

I felt my womb empty itself
and I think,
it took a part of my heart with it.
I'm forever broken, missing pieces.

-Miscarriage

You fill the bucket that's already full,
because it's easier for you,
than to look at the one that's empty.

Something happens inside of you,
when you see a person die.
It's not obvious at first,
but when you lock eyes with that person
in their last seconds of life,
before they leap 50 meters to their death,
you feel fear and guilt
that you weren't able to stop them
no matter how young you might have been.
The sadness and loneliness in their eyes,
their soul, all of that nice little package
floats in the air and gets transferred over to you,
cursing you with the same feelings for eternity.

-Luminous Veil suicide, 1997

I told you the most intimate
details and thoughts
about myself
and you exposed them
for everyone to see.

You said you would never hurt me,
but then you turned around
and emptied me of myself.

A life giving body
is useless
to the ones who
can't produce fruit.

-Infertility

This entire time
I've been sitting at this table,
surrounded by all these people.
Everyone is talking and every plate is full.
I'm seated in the middle,
my plate is empty
and I'm starving.
Yet, no one seems to notice
because I'm smiling.

-The mask

She's drowning and no one is there to save her.
There is never any water;
her own body is drowning her.
Poisoning her to death,
with a black venom that seeps through her veins.
It comes out of her so visibly, that it scares people off.
They don't want to get close to her,
don't want to touch her, help her, or even save her.

She has an invisible disease,
but her symptoms leave marks all over her body.

A barren mother,
is still barren
forever.

-Empty womb

I'm a candle that keeps trying to ignite,
but the wind keeps killing my light.

-Trying my best

Even when I'm weak,
I want to stand.
Instead of encouraging me,
you force me down
and tell me to sit it out
while you stand in my place.

You treat me like an annoying shit smelling fly,
when I'm really a honey making bee.

You called yourself my angel,
but you made me doubt heaven.

I held on to you for too long
and got burned.

Invisible pain
and suffering
are some of the hardest things to survive.

-No one knows it but you

You have two servings on your plate,
I have nothing on mine.
How can you tell me that you know
what starving is like?

-Mental health awareness

Sadness and anger,
Are closely linked together.
But sometimes I wonder,
do you need space or should I come closer?

There was a time when
we didn't know what
we'd gotten ourselves into;
a time when
we just wanted to quit.

If a boat
doesn't float
is it still a boat?
If a woman
is barren,
is she still a woman?

Every month it's the same,
my body's rejection game.
A comedy show, to which I am privy.
My infertility laughs at me.
It promises to do better next time,
not a no, just not this time.
But I've heard that line before
and I collapse on the floor.

-Period

For me you've been both,
a dry log and a rush of water.
Both igniting and putting out my fire.
You calm me but you anger me.
I love you and I hate you.
You get me but you don't know me.
You inspire me but you discourage me.
You're the rainforest to my desert,
but the thorn to my rose.
You're as delicious as chocolate cake,
but your sugar makes me ill.
You're a best friend and the enemy.
You're good when I'm evil
and bad when I'm an angel.
You're my best motivation,
but my worst competition;
the Cat to my Deere.
My strength when I fear,
the keeper of my terrors.
The hand that saves me,
the grip that chokes me.
The feet that guide me
but the path that loses me.

Our souls
are linked
since the day we met.
But I need to let go of you,
to get back to me.
Yet, if I release you from me,
I will lose a part of my soul with it
and it will remain yours forever.

You're my white knight
in battered armor;
fighting the dark storm,
conquering my demons.
I'm the dark angel
in winged splendor,
hitting your form
stealing your freedom.

They give us hope,
just when they start to sense that we've lost all of ours.
They poke us awake,
when we're ready to go to sleep.
They drag us on a desert path,
when we just want to stop for a drink of water.

-Adoption agencies

I said *no, I'm not ready*,
you said *don't you trust me?*
Then you left.
How could you do that to me?
Did you forget about me?
I'm right where you left me.

Michelle Young

You cleaned my wounds
and stitched them;
gave me the blade
told me where to find them.

They told us it was near impossible.
They said it would probably never happen for us.
They had said it might not survive
and they were right.

-Never saw your face

These scars are the reason I'm still alive,
but they are also the reason I've lost my reason to live.

-Forever missing pieces

I memorized every detail of your face.
I thought you were an angel sent from heaven,
But when you smiled, your eyes didn't.
Instead, they turned black like a raven's.

I feel like I'm trapped, but I've created my own cage. There's no shame in infertility, yet I can't help but whisper the word and cringe at the thought of it. Like a dirty word, it rolls off my tongue in an embarrassed manner. Like I'm disgusted at my own situation and my own body, for failing me.

You said you were trying to fix me,
but I was never broken
or yours to fix.

My distance from you is not personal.
You just remind me of a time
and of the person
I used to be and didn't like.

To appreciate the light,
you must first
respect the dark.

The weather matches my mood. The clouds are heavy and dark. As if a storm is about to erupt. There are no sun rays visible through the clouds, only far away sheets of misty rain in the distance. Music blaring. I feel the familiar poison seeping through my veins, the cancer of the soul that is depression. As the poison clouds my mind with dark thoughts of bottomless falls and constant failures, anxious thoughts and lost hopes, a black viscous liquid envelops the last cell of my cut up heart and squeezes it until I can no longer breathe.

I've tried to push you away from me.
I've moved, changed my name and blocked you.
But it's at night,
when I close my eyes
that I see you.

-You're still there

I trusted you,
because I loved you.
I should have listened
when people said
that love is blind.

She has bottles of cream
in every room,
but her hands
are always dry.

Michelle Young

Your eyes turned red
whenever you got in my head.
Your fists turned white,
when they smashed the wall.
Your words turned to poison,
etched inside my brain.

They don't know what it's like,
walking by that empty room every night.
They don't feel what we feel,
in their eyes it's no big deal.
Meanwhile, our lives have been turned upside down
and we'll never be able to turn it around.

-Empty nursery

Afraid to tell you I'm fine;
that you'll read between the lines.
I really hoped this time was it.
My friends just don't seem to get it.
Hopeful, they tell us to keep trying,
I smile and nod, but inside I'm dying.

-Negative pregnancy test

I saw you running like a fox in the night;
low to the earth, you didn't make a sound.
But your paws left marks on the ground.

When I have dark days,
or feel bad about myself,
that's when I see you in my dreams,
because you think I still need you.

You're the woodpecker
and I am the tree.
You feed off for free,
not knowing you're slowly killing me.
When I'm out of food for you,
you fly to another tree.
But I'm fixed in place,
waiting for the rot to set in.
So the wind can blow me around
and I can finally lay down.
Until another tree can replace me.

-Used

Michelle Young

You gave me the knife by the handle,
I took it by the blade.

I can't stand to see fresh hope in their eyes.
It makes me feel even worse inside.
I can't tell them what I know to be true,
that it's forever going to be only me and you.

Michelle Young

Does it please you to see,
all the damage you've left inside of me?
Are you pleased with your invisible art?
The scars left on my heart.

No amount of "I love you'" and "I'm proud of you",
will change the years of black and blue.
People don't ever change.
No amount of time can do that.
They just learn to hide their true self better.

We often notice stains
better on a white shirt;
dirt shows up darker on the lighter color.

Going through the motions,
but not really here.
My body is functioning,
but my mind is still sleeping
far away,
somewhere else.

-Lost

Loving many
has never been my problem;
loving the right one is.

Pain makes you very aware
of your existence.

My mouth
might be quiet,
but my mind
is too loud
to hear.

I ignored you so well,
for so long,
that when I finally wanted to forgive you,
you were already long gone.

The best thing
I ever did,
was walk away.

The worst thing
I ever did,
was look back.

I see love
and miracles,
but instead
I believe lies.

Michelle Young

You painted invisible scars
on me when I was
a blank canvas.
And now the color of it
doesn't match my house.

I want to invite you in
and ask you to stay,
but the demons that live here
are bound to attack your light.

I was already
in pain and bleeding
when they told us
the results were negative.

My whole life has been a joke;
sarcasm I took as a compliment.

Your mouth
may look sweet,
but your words
are rotten.

You're pretending to be nice to me,
but you're only keeping tabs on me.
You want to test me,
to see if you still have control over me.

A tree fell in the forest
and I saw it.
It was never a question of its existence,
but of mine.

Before the storm,
all is quiet and no one moves.
Once it's over,
you can't quiet
the rain still falling from the leaves,
long after the clouds
have stopped emptying their shadows.

You clipped my wings,
told me to fly.
It never occurred to you,
I needed them to survive.

Too tired to fight the darkness,
I lay down in the light of day,
knowing the shadows will come and have their way.
They attack best in the stillness.
Easy prey, they stick to me;
too tired of fighting, my heavy armor beside me.
Knowing they will attack,
even when I've turned my back;
the darkness feeds off moments of weakness.

Michelle Young

Like a loose string on a sweater,
I keep pulling at it trying to fix it.
But instead, it leaves a hole and destroys it.

This house I live in,
so big I get lost.
It was so small when I found it,
now there are rooms I've forgotten existed.
I've stored stuff in them and locked the key.
Thinking I'd be safe and no one would see,
just how messy my house actually is,
when you look past the rooms I've let you in.
I haven't opened up those rooms in years,
afraid of drowning in all the tears.
I've locked them up behind those walls
but they're trying to escape.

-If walls could talk

I used to see myself as strong
until you unveiled my weaknesses
and placed them in front of me.
Now they're all I can see.

Nobody seems to get it,
no one seems to see it.
But you killed my spirit
and a part of me died with it.
How can they ignore it?

Flat stomach and you're envied,
by those who can no longer wear jeans.
Stomachs so round, it's hard to get around,
so they complain all over town.

I see beauty in their growing belly,
a gift of life to which I'm not privy.
For I'd trade with you my flat tummy,
any day to be a mommy.

Stranded in the dark with my bow and arrow,
aiming at the target in front of me that I can't see.
Releasing it towards the light you bring in when you open the
door.

When a flood hits your home,
all that you've worked for is destroyed;
your things displayed on your lawn.
It's not safe inside,
no place to hide.

No one photographs
the one who takes pictures of everyone else.

-Ghost

Michelle Young

I'm that broken piece of glass,
you falsely took as a precious stone;
but my edges left your flesh cut up.

You fly in and out of my life as you please,
thinking your presence doesn't ruffle any leaves.
It takes me months to clean up the mess you leave behind,
each time you stop in just to say hi.

LIGHT

I look up searching for answers,
even though I know
they are already inside of me.

For years you had me locked in a cage,
Playing games with me;
lion and lamb.
Then I realized that if I was caged,
I was the lion, not the lamb.

-You didn't want me free

I might seem small and useless,
but I have the potential
to grow like a seed.

The sun lit up my path,
where the rain muddied it.
But the sun burned me,
where the rain healed me.

The slower and simpler you live your life,
the more things you'll experience.

True freedom comes from knowing yourself,
not the false version people label you with.

I will let him have his way tonight.
I will gather my strength to fight back.
I will sharpen my arrows
and practice my aim, so I don't miss the target.
So tonight I sleep knowing he'll find me,
but rested and ready I'll be,
when he wakes me.

My sacrifices might go unnoticed and unappreciated,
like a fallen tree still provides shelter and food
to the forest around it;
but eventually the acorns that fall off of me
will grow into new life around me.

Never smart enough for you,
until I found
my own way
and surpassed you.

I write to process what I don't understand;
I write to remember what I wish I could; and
I write to heal myself because no one ever could.

-Learning disabilities

We are
what we tell ourselves
we are.

You pull me up from the ground where I've been laying
and tell me there's nowhere you'd rather be, so you're
staying.
No matter how much I try to push you away,
you keep coming back, to help me find my way.

I stared the devil in the face,
but faced God on my knees.

I'm inspired by
what most people find ugly
and call different.
I find it beautiful
to be uniquely yourself.

I'm the poison in your cup;
you're the sugar in my coffee.

You were a tall tower,
that kept getting bigger,
each time you got meaner,
and thought you were better.
But instead of fearing your power,
I started being nicer;
tempering the ground around you with water,
so you kept growing bigger.
But the ground became softer,
and you started to lean further,
until you stood no longer.

I want more for myself,
than what I've allowed for myself.
I have dreams bigger than my mind can grasp,
that I don't want to let pass.
I have fears that trip me along the way,
but hope to help me surpass the day.

She has over 12 kinds of tea
in her pantry,
but she still buys her coffee
at the local coffee shop.

I'm not insane,
but I'm completely, out of my mind crazy.

Michelle Young

You left me alone
in the dark,
to find my way
back to the light.

So free it feels,
to feel the sun warming my face;
to feel the breeze cooling my skin;
to hear a song bird loud and free;
to see the trees dancing gracefully.
So amazing it feels,
to hold you close to my heart
and know you're near me;
that you're mine and I am yours
and that we are free and rich to be together.

I'll do it because I want to,
but also
because you told me I couldn't.

We drive on
with a muddy window
no idea what lies ahead.

-Faith

I always thought it was strange to say
here goes nothing,
when what we really mean is
here goes everything.

I'm bruised and covered in scars
but I'm not broken.
I won't forget them once they've faded away.
Instead, I will use them as weapons and remember them as battle wounds.
They will remind me of a time I fought against the evil things, you once made me believe about myself.

Just like the clouds
look lighter after it rains,
crying helps heal you
after the pain.

-Healing

Willingness to try
is a success
on its own.

Your smile is like a candle;
it's small, but when the power goes out,
it lights up the entire room.

Facing fear
and trying anyway,
is a small but meaningful victory
for self-appreciation
and development.

I might be damaged,
But that has increased
my value.

-My pain can help others

The light woke me up,
where the dark laid me down.

When you feel lost,
look within yourself;
The answer is always there.
But if it still doesn't make sense,
look around you,
at the trees;
at the stars;
at the waves;
at the mountains;
at the sun;
and the moon.

Like an old piece of paper,
he used her up,
then crumpled her
and threw her out.

You found her amongst the rubbish,
picked her up and smoothed her out.
The wrinkles are still there,
but they're fading out.

Michelle Young

You left me alone
thinking I'd get lost.
But it was this way
that I found myself.

He crushed me into a million tiny pieces.
You walked through all those sharp edges.
You weren't frightened at my hurdles.
You said:
broken glass may cut but it still sparkles.

He lured me to his cage with a purr,
but when I reached out to pet his fur,
he turned around
and pushed me down.
He turned his back,
thinking he had me done,
but I fought back
and won.

Trying to blow out a fire,
might just make it bigger.

You wrapped your scrawny fingers around my wrist,
like a snake around my neck.
I thought you were special like jewelry
until you started suffocating me.

Your *yes* means *no*,
I never know which way to go.
My *no* means <u>*no*</u>,
but you think it means *go*.

I have a ghost that preys on me;
not when I'm weak,
not when I'm strong.
It lives inside me,
like a disease that keeps returning
from remission,
it haunts me from within.

I've learned to both fear and admire
the waves and the fire.
How they destroy and give life,
how we use them to survive,
how powerful and beautiful
and how terrifying they are.

Michelle Young

The invisible scars
he marked on me,
will never fade
but come out in my words.

We could have moved away from each other
to sit in the empty seats next to us.
Instead we stayed in our original seats,
cozied up to each other,
comforted by the closeness of another human being, as if the
slightest movement
would make the world stop.

-Passengers on the bus

Making things
makes me happy,
because
it allows me to create
beautiful things
to put out into
this ugly world.

You learn the most
about yourself
when you're
scared, alone and
in need of something.

Walking and driving nowhere in particular,
allows your mind to wander
and resolves things you ponder.
The results can be spectacular.

I write how I feel
because I've lost my voice
from screaming.
My tears and my blood
have dried up.

-Therapy

Michelle Young

Only once I realized
I was weak,
did I become strong.

Failure doesn't scare me
as much as not trying does.

Michelle Young

There's only one you.
Who would be you,
if you tried to be
just like everybody else?

If you pull back your strive,
we might just survive.
If you pull back your arrows,
leave the past in the shadows,
we can move in the right direction.
Even rocks can become perfection.
We are rare, and just like diamonds,
we won't break under pressure.

-Under pressure

Michelle Young

There's a pure joy
that comes with finding sameness
with another person,
even though all of us are in a constant
fight for our uniqueness.

I am the shadow
and you are the sun.
You tell me to leave,
because I'm blocking the light.
But if there's a shadow,
it's because it was created by the sun.

There will always be darkness in the world.
The key to survive,
is to look for the light.

You tried to drown me
with your words,
but I was born in water.

When you've been hurt,
it's ok to cry,
it's ok to be angry,
it's ok to feel the pain.

But it's never ok
to hurt someone.

-Not your coping method

Raise your children
to respect others,
to love others as they love themselves,
to remember their values
and to dream big.

-Parents

We are so often focused
on the acquisitions,
that we often overlook
the consequences of those actions.

Being happy
with what I have
has been my most important lesson.

Michelle Young

I may take a different way,
I may not do it like you,
but don't for a second think
that I'm not just as capable as you.

The clouds may hide the sun for a while,
but it only takes a little wind to make it bright again.

Michelle Young

I believe in invisible things,
like love and the wind.
Just like a bird doesn't rely on the branch but its own wings.

When you slow down or get closer,
things seem to get clearer.

Pay attention to what gets your heart pumping, because it's either worth pursuing or fearing.

I was sleeping in the shade,
when I should have been enjoying the sun.

It takes both rain and sun
for a seed to grow into a flower.

A heavy rain
can speed up plant growth
and help flowers bloom.

And so a dove fell in love with a crow;
or so, the story goes.

Michelle Young

Saying that words don't hurt,
is like saying fire doesn't burn.

Exploring the past is fine,
but don't build your house there.

Michelle Young

Scars are survival stories
etched on the skin.

You exist for a purpose.
Maybe even simply to breathe for the flowers.

I've built a place to put behind
the things I used to hide,
the things that used to be
everything that consumed me.
I've buried them here for all to see,
you reading these scars of mine, heals me.

I'm a devil with wings;
an angel with horns.
Never one or the other;
black or white.
But both together;
dark and light.

ABOUT THE AUTHOR

Michelle Young lives in Ottawa, ON.
This is her first book.

www.ingramcontent.com/pod-product-compliance
Lightning Source LLC
Chambersburg PA
CBHW070114070426
42448CB00039B/2727